Purce

John F. Runciman

Alpha Editions

This edition published in 2024

ISBN 9789362927552

Design and Setting By

Alpha Editions

www.alphaedis.com

Email - info@alphaedis.com

As per information held with us this book is in Public Domain.
This book is a reproduction of an important historical work.
Alpha Editions uses the best technology to reproduce historical work
in the same manner it was first published to preserve its original nature.
Any marks or number seen are left intentionally to preserve.

Contents

CHAPTER I	- 1 -
CHAPTER II	- 10 -
CHAPTER III	- 17 -
CHAPTER IV	- 25 -
CHAPTER V	- 39 -
LIST OF WORKS.	- 42 -

CHAPTER I

We once had a glorious school of composers. It departed, with no sunset splendour on it, nor even the comfortable ripe tints of autumn. The sun of the young morning shone on its close; the dews of dawn gleam for ever on the last music; the freshness and purity of the air of early morning linger about it. It closed with Purcell, and it is no hyperbole to say the note that distinguishes Purcell's music from all other music in the world is the note of spring freshness. The dewy sweetness of the morning air is in it, and the fragrance of spring flowers. The brown sheets on which the notes are printed have lain amongst the dust for a couple of centuries; they are musty and mildewed. Set the sheets on a piano and play: the music starts to life in full youthful vigour, as music from the soul of a young god should. It cannot and never will grow old; the everlasting life is in it that makes the green buds shoot. To realise the immortal youth of Purcell's music, let us make a comparison. Consider Mozart, divine Mozart. Mixed with the ineffable beauty of his music there is sadness, apart and different from the sadness that was of the man's own soul. It is the sadness that clings to forlorn things of an order that is dead and past: it tinkles in the harpsichord figurations and cadences; it makes one think of lavender scent and of the days when our great-grandmothers danced minuets. Purcell's music, too, is sad at times, but the human note reaches us blended with the gaiety of robust health and the clean young life that is renewed each year with the lengthening days.

The beauty of sanity, strength, and joyousness—this pervades all he wrote. It was modern when he wrote; it is modern to-day; it will be modern to-morrow and a hundred years hence. In it the old modes of his mighty predecessors Byrde and Tallis are left an eternity behind; they belong to a forgotten order. Of the crabbedness of Harry Lawes there is scarcely a trace: that belonged to an era of experiments. The strongest and most original of his immediate predecessors, Pelham Humphries, influenced him chiefly by showing him the possibility of throwing off the shackles of the dead and done with. The contrapuntal formulas and prosaic melodic contours, to be used so magnificently by Handel, were never allowed to harden and fossilise in Purcell's music. Even where a phrase threatens us with the dry and commonplace, he gives it a miraculous twist, or adds a touch of harmony that transforms it from a dead into a living thing, from something prosaic into something poetic, rare and enchanting. Let me instance at once how he could do this in the smallest things. This is ordinary enough; it might be a bit of eighteenth-century counterpoint:

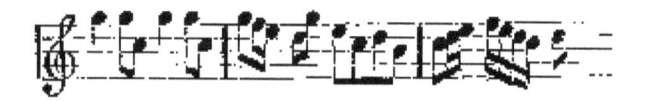

But play it with the second part:

The magic of the simple thirds, marked with asterisks, is pure Purcell. And it is pure magic: there is no explaining the effect. He got into his music the inner essence that makes the external beauty of the picturesque England he knew. That essence was in him; he made it his own and gave it to us. He did not use much of the folk-songs born of our fields and waters, woods and mountains, and the hearts of our forefathers who lived free and did not dream of smoky cities and stinking slums; though folk-song shaped and modified his melodies. In himself he had the spirit of Nature, and it made his music come forth as it makes the flowers blow. The very spirit of the earth seemed to find its voice through him, the spirit of storm and the spirit of fair weather that sports when sweet rains make a musical clatter among the leaves. The music in which he found a voice for Nature cannot grow old while the earth renews its youth with each returning spring. In its pathos and in its joy the soul of seventeenth-century England is in his music in perennial health.

This is not a fanciful description: it is the plainest, most matter-of-fact description. Purcell's music has the same effect on the mind as a crowd of young leaves shooting from a branch in spring; it has a quality of what I risk calling green picturesqueness, sweet and pure, and fresh and vigorous. It is music that has grown and was not made. That Purcell knew perfectly well what he was doing we realise easily when we turn to the music he set to particular words. Take *The Tempest* music, and turn to the song "Arise, ye subterranean winds." See how the accompaniment surges up in imperious, impetuous strength. Turn to "See, the heavens smile": note how the resonant swinging chords and that lovely figure playing on the top give one an instant vision of vast, translucent sea-depths and the ripples lapping above. Look at "Come unto these yellow sands" and "Full fathom five": he almost gives us the colour of the sea and the shore. These things did not come by accident, nor do they exist only in an enthusiastic fancy. They were meant; they are there; and only the deaf and the stupid, or those over-steeped in the later classical music, can help feeling them.

Purcell, then, was the last of the English musicians. So fair and sweet a morning saw the end that many good folk have regarded the end as the beginning, as only the promise of an opulent summer day. How glorious the day might have been had Purcell lived, no one can say; but he died, and no great genius has arisen since. As for the cathedral organists who followed him chronologically, the less said about them the better. What kind of composers they were we can with sorrow see in the music they wrote; what skill as executants they possessed we may judge from the music they played and the beggarly organs they played on. We read of our "great Church musicians"—but these men were not musicians; and of the rich stores of Church music—but, however vast its quantity, it is not, properly speaking, music. The great English musicians who wrote for the Church before Purcell's time were Tallis, Byrde, Whyte, Orlando Gibbons, and they composed not for the English, but for the Roman Church. When I say that Pelham Humphries and Purcell were not religious at all, but purely secular composers, thoroughly pagan in spirit, I imply—or, if you like, exply—that the Church of England has had no religious musicians worth mentioning. Far be it from me to doubt the honest piety of the men who grubbed through life in dusty organ-lofts. Their intentions may have been of the noblest, and they may have had, for all I or anyone can know, sincere religious feeling. But they got no feeling whatever into their intolerably dreary anthems and services; and as for their intentions, the cathedrals of England might be paved with them.

Tallis has often been called "the father of English Church music." If his ghost ever wanders into our cathedral libraries, let us hope he is proud of his progeny. He, like his contemporaries, was a Catholic, and he dissembled. About his birth it has only been conjectured that he was born in the earlier part of the sixteenth century. He was organist of Waltham Abbey in 1540, and remained there till the dissolution of the monasteries, when he became a Gentleman of the Chapel Royal. He and Byrde in 1575 got a patent giving them a monopoly of the printing of music and of music paper, and they printed their own works, which it is a good thing publishers abstain from doing nowadays. In 1585 he died. He was a fine master of polyphony, and as a genuine composer is second only to Byrde. William Byrde, however, stands high above him and all other composers of the time. He was born about 1538, and died in 1623. His later life would have been full of trouble, and the noose or the flames at the stake might have terminated it, if powerful patrons had not sheltered him. The Nonconformist conscience was developing its passion for interfering in other people's private concerns. Byrde, to worship as he thought fit, and to avoid the consequences of doing it, had often to lie in hiding. But he got safely through, and composed a large quantity of splendid Church music, besides some quite unimportant secular music. His masses have a character of their own, and in his motets one finds not only a high degree of technical skill, power and sheer beauty, but also a positive white heat of passion curiously kept from breaking out. There were many others of smaller or greater importance, and the school of English religious composers, properly so called—the men who wrote true devotional music—ended with Orlando Gibbons in 1625. Since then we have had no religious musicians. The Catholic Church brought them forth, and when that Church suffered eclipse we got no more of them.

Not that music was at all eclipsed. The last great English musician was not born till more than a hundred years after the Reformation. Between Gibbons and Purcell came, amongst others, John Jenkins, Henry Lawes, Matthew Locke, Pelham Humphries, Dr. Blow, Captain Cooke and the madrigal writers. These last, however, mainly used contrivances adapted from sacred music. Some really beautiful madrigals exist, but Purcell could have done almost if not quite as well without them. During this period the old style of polyphonic music went out and the new came in. To understand the change, I beg the reader to refrain from impatience under the infliction of a few technicalities; they are a regrettable but inexorable necessity.

The old polyphonic music differed from the newer harmonic music in three respects:

1. *Form and Structure.*—Nearly all the important old music, the music that counts, was for voices—for chorus—with or without accompaniment. "Forms," in the modern sense of the word—cyclical forms with recurring themes arranged in regular sequence, and with development passages, etc.—of these there were none. Some composers were groping blindly after a something they wanted, but they did not hit on it. Self-sustaining musical structures, independent of words, were poor and flimsy. The form of the music that matters was determined by the words. From beginning to end of each composition voice followed voice, one singing, higher or lower, what had been sung by the others, while those others added melodies that made correct harmony. Thus a web of music was spun which has to be listened to, so to speak, horizontally and vertically—horizontally for the melodies that are sung simultaneously, and vertically for the chords that are produced by the sounding together of the notes of those melodies. When the words were used up the composition came to an end. Often the words were repeated, and repeated often; but there should be reason in all things, and the finest composers stopped when they had finished.

The tendency in the new music was to abandon the horizontal aspect. Purcell, in his additions to Playford's "Brief Introduction to the Skill of Musick," remarks on the fact that musicians now composed "to the treble, when they make counterpoint or basses to tunes or songs." Music became, broadly speaking, tunes with an accompaniment. The fugue was no contradiction of this. Even in its heyday, though the parts were ever so independent of one another, the mass of tone forms a great melody, or *melos*, moving on a firm harmonic foundation in the lowest part. The great choral fugues of Bach and Handel have often in the accompaniment a bass moving independently of the bass voice part, and this instrumental bass was figured so that the harmonies could be filled in, on the organ.

2. *Melody*.—There was fine melody enough in the old music, but its rhythm was very subtle, and there was no suggestion of catchiness in it. Melody of a familiar folk-song or dance type now came in, divided into regular periods with strongly-marked rhythms. This may be seen clearly in, for example, Morley's "ballets"—part-songs that could be danced to. Clear, easily understood, when once it came in it, never went out again. Its shaping power may be felt in the fugue subjects of Bach and Handel, as well as in their songs. This folk-song type of melody was modified during the search after expressive declamation. The ideal was to get tunes which were beautiful as tunes, and at the same time did full justice to the composer's words, to preserve the accent and full meaning of the poetry. Henry Lawes won Milton's approbation by his success in doing this, and Milton wrote:

> "Harry, whose tuneful and well-measured notes
> First taught our English music how to span
> Words with just note and accent."

Lawes was not always successful: when his tunes do not disregard the words they are apt to be angular.

3. *Harmony*.—- When a modern person first hears a piece of accompanied plainsong sung, he is generally bewildered. The beginning may trouble him and the middle worry him—the ending invariably confounds him. The thing ends in no key recognised by the modern ear. In the old days there were no keys, but modes, each with its dominant, its tonic, and proper and appropriate ending. Until comparatively recent times musicians understood this quite well; to Purcell, and to composers much later than him, the old endings were perfectly satisfactory. This, for instance, left no sense of the unfinished:

Gradually two keys swamped and swept away the modes—our major and minor; then our modern feeling for key relationships was born. Here is the major scale of C with a satisfactory harmonic ending:

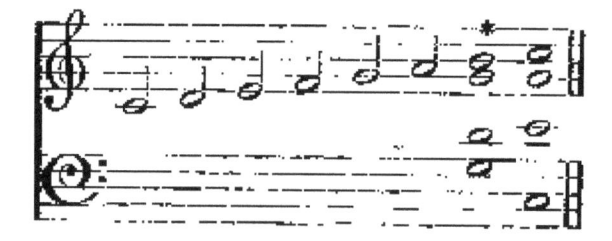

It will be noticed that the top note of the chord marked with a star, the last note but one of the scale, is a semitone below the last note of the scale and rises to the last note. That is a proper ending or full close; what was called a half-close was:

As a termination to a piece of music made up of the notes of the scale of C, and therefore said to be in the key of C, this was not satisfactory. To set the ear and the mind at ease, to get a feeling that the music has settled down on a secure resting-place, the first chord had to be repeated. And in these chords

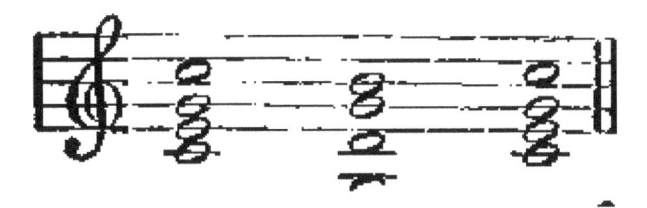

lies the germ of the whole of the later music. Only two more steps were needed. By adding an F, or writing an F instead of the upper G in the middle chord, the chord of the dominant seventh was obtained:

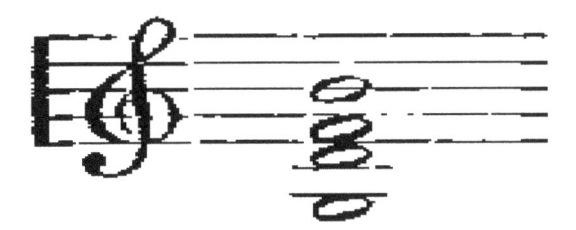

And anyone can try for himself on a piano, and find out that this chord makes the longing for the tonic chord—the chord of C—more imperious and the feeling of rest satisfying in proportion when the last chord is reached. That was one step: the next was to convert the dominant, G, of the key of C into a tonic for the time being, to get a sense of having reached the key of G. That was done by regarding G as a tonic, and on *its* dominant, D, writing a chord, either a dominant seventh or a simple major common chord, leading to a chord of G—thus:

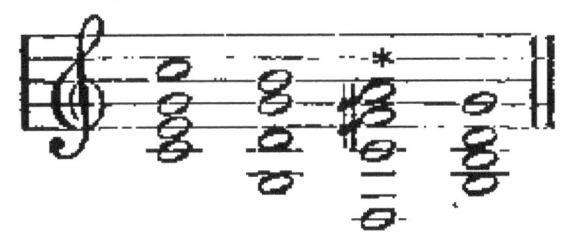

But if after this a seventh on the dominant is played, followed by the original key-chord then we are home once more in the original key. If the reader will imagine, instead of a few simple chords, a passage of music in the key of C, followed by a passage in the dominant key of G, and ending with a passage in the key of C, he will perceive that here is the deep underlying principle of modern music: that after a certain length of time spent in one key the ear wearies, and the modulation to the new key is grateful; but after a time the ear craves for the original key again, so after getting to that, and spending a certain time there, a piece closes with perfectly satisfying effect. Haydn was the first to get that principle in an iron grasp and use it, with numberless other devices, to get unity in variety. Not till nearly a hundred years after Purcell's day did that come to pass; but the music of Purcell and of others in his period, showing a sense of key relationships and key values, is a vast step from the music written in the old modes. Let me beg everyone not to be so foolish as to believe the nonsense of the academic text-books when they speak of the new type and structure of the newer music as an "improvement" on the old. The older were perfect for the things that had to be expressed; the newer became necessary only when other things had to be expressed. By the substitution of the two scales, the major and the minor, with the dominant always on the same degree of the scale, the fifth, and the order of the tones and semitones fixed immovably, for the numerous modes with the dominants and the order of the tones and semitones here, there and everywhere, the problems of harmony could be grappled with, and its resources exploited in a methodical way that had been impossible. But melodically the loss was enormous. We of this generation have by study to win back some small sense of the value and beauty of the intervals of the ancient scales, varying in each scale, a sense that was once free and common to everyone who knew anything of music at all.

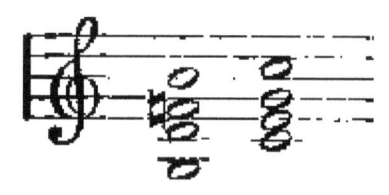

Purcell and his immediate predecessors and contemporaries came into what Hullah rightly called the "transition period." Purcell is now to be considered, and of the others it need only be said that we see in their music the old modes losing their hold and the new key sense growing stronger. Their music compared with the old is modern, though compared with all music later than Handel it is archaic.

PURCELL.

(From a portrait by Closterman, in the
National Portrait Gallery.)

CHAPTER II

What we know of Purcell's life is nothing, or next to nothing; what is written as his life is conjecture, more or less ingenious inference, or pure fiction. In that we know so little of him he is blessed, but the blessedness has not as yet extended to his biographers. At one time a biographer's task was easy: he simply took the hearsay and inventions of Hawkins, and accepted them as gospel truth whenever they could not be tested. The fact that whenever they could by any means be tested they were found to be false—even this did not dismay the biographer. Hawkins's favourite pastime was libelling the dead. He libelled Dr. Johnson, and Boswell promptly and most vigorously dealt with him; he libelled Purcell grossly—he deliberately devised slanderous tales of him. The biographers, with simple, childlike credulity, went on whenever possible repeating his statements, for the obvious reason that this course was the easiest. Hawkins knew nothing of Purcell. He can be proved to be wrong, not merely about this or that detail, but about everything. He is said to have known one Henry Needler, a pupil of Purcell, and also Gostling, the son of the singer of the same name for whom Purcell wrote; but neither acquaintance seems to have profited him aught. His anecdotes are the product of inborn wickedness and an uncouth, boorish imagination. When we have cleared away his garbage, there remains only a skeleton life, but at any rate we have the satisfaction of knowing that is pure fact.

Henry Purcell was born (probably) about the end of 1658, and (probably also) in Westminster. Some of his family were musicians before him. His father, Henry Purcell the elder, was a Gentleman of the Chapel Royal (that is, a singer in the choir, and in many cases organist as well), and was master of the choristers at Westminster Abbey for three years. He held various posts in the "King's Musick," sharing the duties of "lute and voyce" for a time with one Angelo Notari. The latter appears to have died in 1663; but strangely enough after his death he asked for arrears of salary for 1661 and 1664. However, in 1663 Henry Purcell the elder seemed to have taken over the whole duties of their joint post; and he, Purcell, died in 1664. If Henry the younger was six years old at the time of his father's death, then he must have been born in 1658 or, at latest, the early part of 1659; if he was born in 1658 or the early part of 1659, then he must have been six years old at the time of his father's death. So much we know positively; anything more is supposition—that is, the whole affair is supposition; but this supposition has one merit: it cannot be very widely wrong. Pepys knew Henry the elder, and refers to him in his Diary; and it may be remarked in passing that those who wish to grow familiar with the atmosphere in which Purcell was brought up, and lived and worked, must go to Pepys, who knew all the musicians of the period, and the life of Church, Court, and theatre. Thomas Purcell, brother of Henry the elder, was also a Gentleman of the Chapel Royal. He succeeded Henry Lawes as Court lutanist, and held other positions, and evidently stood high in favour. This Thomas certainly adopted Henry the younger at the death of Henry the elder, and afterwards he wrote of him as "my sonne." Young Henry seems to have become a choir-boy as a mere matter of family custom. He joined as one of "the children" of the Chapel Royal, with Captain Cooke as his master. Cooke must have been a clever musician in spite of the military title he had gained while fighting on the Royalist side in the Civil War. He had an extraordinarily gifted set of boys under him, and he seems to have trained them well. When some of them tried their infantile hands at composition he encouraged them. Pepys heard at least one of their achievements, and records his pleasure. And it must be remembered that Pepys was a composer and connoisseur—he would go many miles to hear a piece of music. Cooke died in 1672, and Pelham Humphries became master of "the children." He was born in 1647, and therefore was eleven years older than Purcell; he, too, had been a child of the Chapel Royal. In 1664 Charles sent him abroad to study foreign methods. In the accounts of the secret-service money for 1664, 1665, and 1666 stand sums of money paid him to defray his expenses; yet in 1665 the accounts of the "King's Musick" show that Cooke received £40 "for the maintenance of Pelham Humphryes." In less than a year's time he was appointed musician for the lute—in the "King's Musick"—in the place of Nicholas Lanier, deceased. Two months after this entry the appointment is confirmed by warrant. He undoubtedly did go abroad. He got, at any rate, as far as Paris, and came back, says Pepys, "an absolute monsieur"—very vain, loquacious, and "mighty great" with the King. Most of the musicians of the time were vain. Cooke must have been intolerable. Perhaps they learnt it from the actors with whom they associated—many of them, in fact, were actors as well as musicians. Humphries had worked under Lulli. It is not known that he had any other master in Paris or in Italy, or whether he ever got as far as Italy. Up to that date no opera of Lulli's seems to have been produced, but he was none the less a master of music, and he could hand on what he had learnt of Carissimi's technique. Humphries, highly gifted, swift, returned to England knowing all Lulli could teach him. He had not Purcell's rich imagination, nor his passion, nor that torrential flow of ever-fresh melody; but it cannot be doubted that he was of immense service in indicating new paths and new ways of doing things. He had—at second hand we must admit— Carissimi's methods and new impulse; and, at the very least, he saved Purcell the trouble of a journey to Paris. It was a misfortune for English music that he died so early. These Restoration geniuses had a way of dying early. He distinctly had genius, a very different thing from the plodding industry of Dr. John Blow, who succeeded him in 1674. Dr. Blow afterwards claimed to have been Purcell's master, and, as Purcell was certainly his pupil, there seems no reason for doubting him. Purcell was, of course, sixteen years of age when Humphries died, and no longer a mere choir-boy; but he remained attached to Westminster Abbey and the Chapel Royal. According to the records of the "King's Musick," on June 10, 1673, there is a "warrant to admit Henry Purcell in the place of keeper, maker, mender, repayrer and tuner of the regalls, organs, virginalls, flutes and recorders and all other kind of wind instruments whatsoever, in ordinary, without fee, to his Majesty, and assistant to John Hingston, and upon the death or other avoydance of the latter, to come in ordinary with fee." So late as 1683, when Purcell had been organist of Westminster Abbey for about three years, he was appointed to be "organ-maker and keeper in the place of Mr. Hingston, deceased." The conjecture of Rev. Henry Cart de Lafontaine, editor of these records (published by Novello) seems to be correct: Purcell must have been apprenticed to Hingston and afterwards succeeded him. In later warrants he is authorised to buy wood, metal and Heaven knows what else—he can buy what he likes as long as he keeps the instruments in order and in tune. Charles II. had a good ear. In 1676 Purcell was appointed "copyist" of Westminster Abbey, whatever post that may have been. In 1677 "Henry Purcell" is "appointed composer in ordinary with fee for the violin to his Majesty, in the place of Matthew Lock, deceased." I fancy that his tuition from Dr. Blow must have been mainly in organ-playing, in which art Dr. Blow was an esteemed master. At the same time, we must not forget that we have Purcell's own word for it that Blow was one of the greatest masters of composition in the world. Purcell spoke of Dr. Blow's technical mastery of the tricks of canon-writing, which Purcell himself was much addicted to, and greatly enjoyed. Dr. Blow may have taught Purcell something of the older technique; that of Lulli and the Italians he must have learnt from Humphries, for Dr. Blow knew next to nothing about it. Dr. Blow was born in 1648, and was one year younger than Humphries, and ten older than Purcell. In 1669 he became organist of Westminster Abbey. He, like Humphries, and, indeed, all the foremost musicians of the period, was a bloated pluralist, and held other positions. It is said that he resigned Westminster Abbey in 1680 in Purcell's favour. Whether the resignation was voluntary or not, Purcell assuredly took his place at that date. After Purcell's death in 1695 Dr. Blow took the position again, and retained it until his own death, in 1708. It is also said that he resigned another place to make way for another pupil, Jeremiah Clarke. This apparent passion or mania for resigning posts in favour of gifted pupils might easily have led to a pernicious custom amongst organists. However, since Dr. Blow's time the organist of Westminster Abbey has always been a more business-like person, though rarely, if ever, a fine artist. Dr. Blow, living amongst men of such genius, caught a little—a very little—of Humphries' and Purcell's lordly manner in the writing of music; but no sweet breath of inspiration ever blew his way. Burney, unfortunate creature, found fault with his harmonies, and these have been defended as "spots on the sun." As a matter of fact, the harmonies are good enough. There are no spots—only there is no sun. His claim to have taught Purcell is a claim for such immortality as books give. Purcell's teacher will be remembered long after the composer of anthems has been crowded out of biographical dictionaries.

I have said that our knowledge of Purcell consists very largely of speculations, hypotheses and inferences. These have led the biographers into wasting some highly moral reflections on Purcell's early doings. We are told, for example, that he composed music for the theatre until he became organist of Westminster Abbey, after which date he applied his energies wholly to the service of the Church. Had the biographers not kindly followed the blind Hawkins and Burney, and hearsay generally, those reflections might have been saved for a more fitting occasion. It was long held that Purcell wrote the incidental music for *Aureng-Zebe*, *Epsom Wells*, and *The Libertine* about 1676, when he was eighteen, because those plays were performed or published at that time. It used to be said that the music, though immature, showed promise, and was indeed marvellous for so young a man. But unless one possesses the touchstone of a true critical faculty and an intimate acquaintance with Purcell's music and all the music of the time, one should be cautious—one cannot be too cautious. The music for these plays was not composed till at least fifteen years later. The biographers had also a craze for proving Purcell's precocity. They would have it that *Dido and Aeneas* dated from his twenty-second year. If they had boldly stuck to their plan of attributing the music to the year of the first performance of the play to which it is attached, they might easily have shown him to have been a prolific composer before he was born. The prosaic truth is that Purcell came before the world as a composer for the theatre in the very year of his appointment to Westminster Abbey, and during the last five years of his life he turned out huge quantities of music for the theatre. It is easy to believe that his first experiments were for the Church. He was brought up in the Church, and sang there; when his voice broke he went on as organist. Some of his relatives and most of his friends were Church musicians. But Church and stage were not far apart at the Court of Charles, and, moreover, the more nearly the music of the Church resembled that of the stage, the better the royal ears were pleased. Pepys' soul was filled with delighted approval when he noticed the royal hand beating the time during the anthem, and, in fact, Charles insisted on anthems he could beat time to. Whilst "on his travels" he had doubtless observed how much better, from his point of view, they did these things in France. There was nothing vague or undecided in that curious mind. He knew perfectly well what he liked, and insisted on having it. He disliked the old Catholic music; he disliked quite as much Puritan psalm-singing—that abominable cacophony which to-day is called "hearty congregational singing." He wanted jolly Church music, sung in time and in tune; he wanted secular, not sacred, music in church. But his taste, though secular, was not corrupt—the music-hall Church music and Salvation Army tunes of to-day would probably have outraged his feelings. His taste coincided with Purcell's own. Along with some of the old-fashioned genuine devotional music, Purcell must have heard from childhood a good deal of the stamp he was destined to write; he must often have taken his part in Church music that might, with perfect propriety, have been given in a theatre. All things were ripe for a secular composer; the mood that found utterance in the old devotional music was a dead thing, and in England Humphries had pointed the new way. Purcell was that secular composer.

One spirit, the secular, pagan spirit, breathes in every bar of Purcell's music. Mid-Victorian critics and historians deplored the resemblance between the profane style of the stage pieces and the sacred style of the anthems and services. Not resemblance, but identity, is the word to use. There is no distinguishing between the two styles. There are not two styles: there is one style—the secular style, Purcell's style. Let us pause a moment, and ask ourselves if any great composer has ever had more than one style. Put aside the fifth-rate imitators who now copied Mozart, and now Palestrina, and could therefore write in as many styles as there were styles to copy, and not one of them their own. There is no difference between the sacred motets and the secular madrigals of the early polyphonists. Bach did not use dance-measures in his Church music, but in the absence of these lies the entire distinction between his Church and his secular compositions; the structure, manner and outlines of his songs are precisely alike—indeed, he dished up secular airs for sacred cantatas. The style of Handel's "Semele" and that of his "Samson" are the same; there is no dissimilarity between Haydn's symphonies and the "Creation"; Mozart's symphonies and his masses (though the masses are a little breezier, on the whole); Schubert's symphonies or songs and his masses or "The Song of Miriam"; Beethoven's Ninth Symphony and the great Mass in D.

Purcell's style is largely a sort of fusion of all the styles in vogue in his lifetime. The old polyphonic music he knew, and he was a master of polyphonic writing; but with him it was only a means to the carrying out of a scheme very unlike any the old writers ever thought of—the interest of each separate part is not greater than the general harmonic interest. Then, as he admitted, he learnt a great deal from the Italians. From Lulli, through Humphries, he got declamatory freedom in the bonds of definite forms, not letting the poet's or the Bible words warp his music out of all reasonable shape. The outlines of his tunes show unmistakably the influence of English folk-song and folk-dance. There was an immense amount of household music in those days—catches, ballads, songs and dances. The folk-songs, even if they were invented before the birth of the modern key-sense, were soon modified by it: very few indications can be found of their having originated in the epoch when the modes had the domination; and the same is true of the dances. The sum of these influences, plus Purcell's innate tendencies, was a style "apt" (in the phraseology of the day) either for Church, Court, theatre, or tavern—a style whose combined loftiness, directness, and simplicity passed unobserved for generations while the big "bow-wow" manner of Handel was held to be the only manner tolerable in great music.

By 1680 Purcell's apprenticeship was at end. Early compositions by him had been published in Playford's "Choice Ayres" in 1676 and 1679; in 1677 he had been appointed "composer (to the King) in ordinary for the violin, in the place of Matthew Lock, deceased"; but none of the highest official posts were his. And we must remember that official position was a very different thing in Restoration times from what it is to-day. Nowadays the world is bigger and more thickly populated, and men of intellect and genius scorn Court appointments and official appointments generally. These are picked up by Court toadies, business-headed persons, men belonging to well-connected families—the Tite Barnacles of the generation. The men of power appeal to the vast public direct. In Purcell's day there was no vast public to appeal to. Concerts had scarcely been devised; no composer could live by publishing his works. The Court, the theatre, the Church—he had to win a position in one or other or all of these if he wished to live at all. So in 1680 Purcell the master passed over the head of his teacher, Dr. John Blow, to the organistship of Westminster Abbey—that is, he was recognised as the first organist living. In the same year he composed the first theatre pieces he is known to have composed—those for Lee's *Theodosius*. (I disregard as fatuous the supposition that in his boyhood he wrote the *Macbeth* music attributed, perhaps wrongly, to Locke.) It was not for some time that he gained the supremacy at the theatre which he now held in the Church. That very trustworthy weathercock John Dryden, Poet Laureate, continued to flatter others for many long days to come. In this same year he composed the first of a long series of odes of welcome, congratulation or condolence for royal or great personages, and about this year he married.

PURCELL SEATED AT THE HARPSICHORD.
(From a portrait by Clostermann, in the National Portrait Gallery.)

CHAPTER III

During the first ten years of his mastership Purcell composed much—precisely how much we can only guess. It was not until 1690 that he began the huge string of incidental theatre sets which were for so long spoken of as his operas. Mr. Barclay Squire, to whom all who are interested in Purcell are deeply indebted, has clearly established that by 1690, though not more than two years earlier, his one opera, *Dido and Aeneas*, was written. If we take this as belonging to the period which began in 1690, we have for these first ten years only ten plays to which he provided music, and of these several are very doubtful, and the rest not very important. During the remaining six years of his life he wrote music for forty-two plays. Several sets are of the greatest importance, amongst them *Dioclesian, King Arthur, The Fairy Queen* and *The Tempest*.

We cannot tell how many of the anthems belong to this period. One might surmise that most of them do, as his activity at the theatre later on must have occupied most of his time. But if we had no dates for Mozart's three greater symphonies, we might readily fall into the mistake of attributing them to another year than that of their composition, and the mistake would be natural, if not inevitable, when we consider the enormous amount of music we know Mozart to have written in 1788. In Purcell we find the same terrific, superhuman energy manifested as the day of his death drew near, and perhaps we may be wrong in imagining that the theatre wholly absorbed him. A few of the anthems may with great probability be ascribed to certain dates because of the royal events with which they are connected. For example, two ("I was Glad," and "My Heart is Inditing") must have been written for the coronation of James II. in 1685. For "the Queen's pregnancy" in 1688 another ("Blessed are They that Fear the Lord") was certainly composed. The anthems for the Queen's funeral—and, as it turned out, for Purcell's own—can also be dated in the same way, but they fall into a later period.

During these ten years fifteen odes were set, including the notable *Yorkshire Feast Song*, also the music for "the Lord Mayor's show of 1682," and the *Quickstep*, which afterwards became famous when the words "Lillibulero" were adapted to it. It was sung as a sort of war-song against James II. In 1687 Purcell wrote an elegy on John Playford, the son of the publisher of the same name.

It would be utterly impossible to determine the dates of upwards of 200 songs, duets, trios, and catches, nor does it greatly matter. In a little book such as this we have little enough space without going into these questions. The first sonatas in three parts are more important. They were published in 1683, with a portrait of the composer at the age of twenty-four. Some pieces for strings in from three to eight parts may be attributed to 1680. Some of the many harpsichord things may also belong to this period.

We cannot follow Purcell's development step by step, year by year, as we can, for instance, Beethoven's. When we come to survey his work as a whole, we shall be able to compare the three-part sonatas issued in 1683 with the sonatas in four parts published in the year after his death. We shall learn that towards the end of his life he was a more magnificent master, than he was when twenty-four years old. That is the most we can see. We may observe ode after ode, it is true, but with regard to them we ought to be able to take into account conditions and limitations of which nothing is recorded nor can be known. This holds, also, with regard to the theatre music. We can merely guess at what his employers asked him to provide. We can never know the means they placed at his disposal. One significant thing must be noted here: the music itself—its style, spirit, even mannerism—affords us no trustworthy clue as to when any particular piece may have been written. For ages the biographical copyists have not ceased to marvel at a boy of fourteen writing the *Macbeth* music. It is silly rubbish, with which I believe Purcell had nothing whatever to do. They marvelled at the immature power latent in the music to *The Libertine*, which they supposed he wrote in 1676. Alas! the date is 1692. They marvelled still more over *Dido and Aeneas*, attributed to 1680. Alas! again its date is much later—1688 to 1690. The evidence of style counts for little. The truth is that in Purcell's music there are no marked stages of development, no great changes in style. Undoubtedly he gradually grew in power, richness of invention, fecundity of resource; but the change was one of degree, not of kind. He never, as Beethoven did, went out to "take a new road." He struck what he knew to be *his* right road at the very beginning, and he never left it. His nature and the point in history at which he appeared forbade that the content of his music should burst the form. The forms he began with served him to the end.

I shall first deal with such of Purcell's compositions as may fairly be considered as having been written before 1690. The music for the dramas is not of an ambitious character. It consists mainly of songs, dances, and "curtain tunes." In many cases half a dozen items are all that are attached to one play, and many of the pieces are brief. Therefore that formidable-looking list of what used to be called Purcell's "operas" does not represent anything like the quantity of music we might suppose. Purcell wrote only one opera—*Dido*. The word "opera" had not in his day acquired a special meaning. Spectacular plays, with songs, duets, choruses, dances, etc., were called entertainments or operas indiscriminately. Until a few daring inquirers investigated, the world supposed Purcell to have collaborated with the playwrights. In a few later shows it is true that he did, but some of the plays were written before he was born, some while he was a boy, and others—later ones—are known to have been first given without the aid of his music. *The Indian Emperour* was first played in 1665; Purcell added music in 1692. *Tyrannic Love* was produced in 1668 or 1669; the music was added in 1694. *The Indian Queen* was produced before *The Emperour*; the music was done in the last year of Purcell's life. If the *Circe* music is indeed Purcell's, it cannot have been written until the author, Davenant, had been in his grave seventeen years. If only the estimable ladies and gentlemen whose passion for writing about Purcell has wrapped the real man in a haze of fairy tales had taken the preliminary trouble of learning a little of the literature and drama of Purcell's day! Nay, had they only looked at the scores of Purcell's "operas"! Most of these plays undoubtedly had some music from the beginning. It will be remembered that during the Puritan, joyless reign of dunderheadedness the playhouses were closed; but Cromwell, who loved music and gave State concerts, licensed Davenant to give "entertainments"—plays in which plot, acting, and everything else were neglected in favour of songs, dances, and such spectacles as the genius and machinery of the stage managers enabled them to devise. When the Puritan rule faded, the taste for these shows still persisted. Dryden took full advantage of this taste, and after 1668 threw songs wholesale into his plays. Further, it would seem to have been the custom of theatre managers, when "reviving" forgotten or half-forgotten plays, to put in new songs and dances and gorgeous scenes, in the very spirit of Mr. Vincent Crummles, as the extra attractions. As Purcell's fame spread, his help would be more and more sought. At first Mr. Crummles would be content with a few simple things, but later, finding these "a draw," he would rely more on Purcell's aid. This is pure speculation, but it is fact that the earlier plays embellished by Purcell have nothing like the quantity of music we find in the later ones. One venturesome biographer, by the way, not only insists on Purcell's authorship of the *Macbeth* music, but suggests that "probably the recognition of the excellence and effectiveness" of such dull stuff "induced the managers of theatres to give him further employment." They were certainly a long time about it, for Lee's *Theodosius*, the first play for which Purcell is known to have composed incidental music, was not produced till 1680, eight years after the latest possible date of the *Macbeth* music; and, apart from *Dido*, which is not a play, but an opera, it was eighteen years till these same astute managers were "induced" by "the excellence and effectiveness" of the *Macbeth* or any other music to give Purcell something serious to do in the theatre. It was in 1690 that *Dioclesian* appeared, the first and one of the most important of a long string of works for the stage. The hypotheses, the "wild surmises" and the daring defiance of mere facts indulged in by biographers are indeed wonderful, as they strive and strain to read and to fill in the nearly obliterated, dim and distant record of Purcell's life. Yet it is risky for a biographer to laugh; perhaps it is utterly wrong to conjecture that towards the end of his life Purcell had become indispensable, and was engaged to supply the music for *all* the plays as they were given, big or little, as they came along. Nor do we know how much more music may have been written for the first plays, nor how much of what has been preserved is genuine Purcell.

On one point we may be quite certain. It is the greatest pity that Purcell wasted so much time on these Restoration shows. When the English people revolted against Puritanism, and gave the incorrigible Stuarts another chance, Charles the Wanderer returned to find them in a May-Day humour. They thrust away from them for a little while the ghastly spiritual hypochondria of which Puritanism was a manifestation, and determined to make merry. But, heigh-ho! the day of Maypoles was over and gone. From the beginning the jollity and laughter were forced, and the new era of perpetual spring festival soon became an era of brainless indecency. Even the wit of the Restoration was bitter, acid, sardonic (as Charles's own death-bed apology for being an unconscionable time a-dying). Generally it was ill-tempered, and employed to inflict pain. And there was not even wit in most of the plays. It is hard to see what even the worst age could discover to laugh at in Shadwell's *Libertine*, the story of Don Juan told in English, and, in a sense, made the most of.

Because of their nastiness, often combined with stupidity, the Restoration dramas will never be resurrected. There is another reason. The glorious Elizabethan era and spirit were gone; the eighteenth century was coming on fast. Dryden and his fellows had noble rules for the construction of plays, and nobler ones for the language that might or might not be used. They derived all their rules, if you please, from "the ancients." Like Voltaire, they reckoned Shakespeare a barbarian with native wood-notes wild. They took his plays and "made them into plays." They improved *The Tempest*, *Timon of Athens*, *The Midsummer Night's Dream*, and goodness knows how many more. Davenant, in search of material for entertainments, began it; Dryden continued it; even Shadwell had his dirty fingers in it. And this matters to us, for some of Purcell's most glorious songs, choruses and instrumental pieces were composed for these desecrations, and can never again be listened to under the conditions he had in his mind.

According to some authorities ("The Dictionary of National Biography" amongst them), the first play handled by Purcell was Lee's *Sophonisba; or, The Overthrow of Hannibal*; according to others, the first was *Theodosius; or, The Force of Love*. Both, however, date not later than 1685, which is near enough for either when there is nothing like conclusive evidence as to which had the priority. The music for the first plays is in no way bound up with the plays. It consists of instrumental pieces and songs literally interpolated. It is likely enough that tunes written for one play were often enough used for another. The pieces were brief, but the unmistakable Purcellian mingling of strength and sweetness is to be found even in such trifles. In 1690 and later Purcell took full advantage of masques which were inserted, the interpolations being sometimes as long as the rest of the play, and artistically of infinitely greater value. For the present he confined himself to less imposing forms, which was certainly what he was engaged to do.

The finest example of the odes of the period is the so-called *Yorkshire Feast Song* (1689). Many of the others are not, for Purcell, extraordinary. They were written for such special occasions, for instance, as the King's return all the way to London from Windsor, or even Newmarket, or the birthday of a Queen, and in one case the birthday of a six-year-old Duke. They consist of overtures, songs, choruses, etc. With one or two exceptions, the structure is Purcell's ordinary. What that structure was we shall see (once for all) in examining some of the later compositions, the only difference observable in the later works being, on the whole, an increased richness and greater breadth of scheme. They are nearly always brilliant, often incisive; there are most lovely melodies; and there are numerous specimens of Purcell's power of writing music, endless in its variety of outline and colour and changing sentiment, on a ground-bass—*i.e.*, a bass passage repeated over and over again until the piece is finished. The instrumentation must have been largely dictated by the instruments placed at his disposal, though we must remember that in days when it was an everyday occurrence for, say, an oboist to play from the violin part save in certain passages, even an apparently complete score is no secure guide as to what the composer meant, and as to how the piece was given under his direction. This remark applies to the scoring of much of the theatre music. The *Theatre Ayres* contain only string parts, and it is nonsense to suppose that in the theatre of that time Purcell had only strings to write for. Purcell wrote in all twenty-two sonatas—twelve in three parts, ten in four. So far as the number of parts is concerned, there is little real difference. In the three-part works one stave serves for both the string bass-player and the harpsichordist; in the four-part ones there are two separate staves, with trifling variations in the two parts. The twelve three-part sonatas were issued, as has been said, in 1683. They are pure, self-sustaining music, detached from words and scenic arrangements; nothing approaching them had been written by an Englishman, nor anything so fine by an Italian. Indeed, in their own particular way they are matched only by the composer's own four-part sonatas published after his death. We must not look for anything like form in the sense that word conveys nowadays; there is no unalterable scheme of movements such as there is in the Haydn symphony, and within each movement there is no first subject, second subject, development and recapitulation. All that had to be worked out nearly a century later. The set forms of Purcell's day were the dances. The principle of Purcell's sonata form is alternate fast and slow movements. Nothing more can be perceived; there is nothing more to perceive. Sometimes he commences with a quick piece; then we have an adagio or some slow dance; then another quick piece. In other cases the order is reversed: a slow movement may be followed by a slower movement. He makes great use of fugue, more or less free, and of imitation, and, of course, he employs ground-basses. The masculine strength and energy, the harsh clashing discords, are not less remarkable than the constant sweetness; and if there is rollicking spring jollity, there are also moments of deepest pathos. There is scarcely such a thing as a dry page. It is true that Purcell avowed that he copied the best Italian masters, but the most the copying amounts to is taking suggestions for the external scheme of his sonatas and for the manner of writing for strings. He poured copiously his streams of fresh and strong melody into forms which, in the hands of those he professed to imitate, were barren, lifeless things. Many of these sonatas might almost be called rhapsodies; certainly a great many movements are rhapsodical. In set forms one has learnt from experience what to expect. In the dance measures and fugues, after a few bars, one has a premonition (begotten of oft-repeated and sometimes wearisome experience) of what is coming, of the kind of thing that is coming; just as in a Haydn or Mozart sonata one knows so well what to expect that one often expects a surprise, and may be surprised if there is nothing to surprise one. But in many of Purcell's largos, for example, the music flows out from him shaped and directed by no precedent, no rule; it flows and wanders on, but is never aimlessly errant; there is a quality in it that holds passage to passage, gives the whole coherence and a satisfying order. Emerson speaks of Swedenborg's faculties working with astronomic punctuality, and this would apply to Purcell's musical faculties. Take a scrappy composer, a short-breathed one such as Grieg: he wrote within concise and very definite forms; yet the order of many passages might be reversed, and no one—not knowing the original—would be a penny the wiser or the worse. There is no development. With Purcell there is always development, though the laws of it lie too deep for us. Hence his rhapsodies, whether choral or instrumental, are satisfying, knit together by some inner force of cohesion.

During these ten years several children were born to Purcell. He had six children altogether. Four died while still babies; two, Edward and Frances, survived him. Edward lived till 1740, leaving a son; Frances married one

Welsted, or Welstead, and died in 1724. Her daughter died two years later. Before the end of the eighteenth century the line of Purcell's descendants seems to have terminated. In 1682 Purcell became an organist of the Chapel Royal, whilst remaining organist of Westminster Abbey. As has already been said, the musicians of this age were pluralists—they had to be in order to earn a decent living, for the salaries were anything but large, and punctuality in payment was not a feature. In 1684 there was a competition at the Temple Church, not between organists, but between organ-builders. The authorities got two builders to set up each an organ, and decided which was the better by the simple plan of hearing them played by different organists and deciding which sounded the better. To any but a legal mind the affair would seem to have resolved itself mainly into a competition between organ-players; but we know how absolutely lost to all sense of justice, fairness, reason and common sense the legal mind is. So Purcell played for Father Smith, and inevitably the organ built by Father Smith was thought the finer. This easy way of solving a difficult problem, though it has so much to recommend it to the legal mind, has fallen into desuetude, and is abandoned nowadays, even in that home of absurdities, the Temple. For the coronation of James II., Purcell superintended the setting-up of an extra or special organ in the Abbey; and for this he was granted £34 12s. out of the secret-service money. In 1689, at the coronation of the lucky gentleman who superseded James, no such allowance appears to have been made; and Purcell admitted the curious to the organ-loft, making a charge and putting it in his pocket. This was too much for the clergy. They regarded the money as theirs, and as Mr. Gladstone, that stout Churchman, said, the Church will give up rather its faith than its money. The Abbey authorities never thought of giving up either, but they threatened Purcell with terrible penalties unless he gave up the money. Almost with a pistol at his head they asked him to give up his money or his post. How the squabble ended no man knows; the conjecture that he 'refunded' the money—*i.e.*, gave it to those it did not belong to—is unsupported.

These are the only scraps of veracious history that come down to us; the other choice bits I take to be exercises in prosaic romance.

PURCELL.

(From an engraving after a portrait by Clostermann in the possession of the Royal Society of Musicians.)

CHAPTER IV

During the last portion of his life (1690-5) Purcell composed a large amount of music, and that is nearly all we know. Of course, he went on playing the organ—that is indubitable. Of course, also, he gave lessons; but it is a remarkable fact that few musicians after his death claimed to have been his favourite pupils or his pupils at all. That he became, as we should say nowadays, conductor at Drury Lane or any other theatre cannot be asserted with certitude, though it is probable. He wrote incidental music for about forty-two dramas, some of the sets of pieces being gorgeously planned on a large scale. He had composed complimentary odes for three Kings; in the last year of his life he was to write the funeral music for a Queen, and the music was to serve at his own funeral. During this last period he wrote his greatest ode, "Hail, Bright Cecilia"; his greatest pieces of Church music, the *Te Deum* and *Jubilate*; and in all likelihood his greatest sonatas, those in four parts. He also rewrote a part of Playford's *Brief Introduction to the Skill of Music*.

It is not my intention to analyse the dramas. No more can be done in the narrow space than give the reader a notion of Purcell's general procedure of filling his space, and the salient characteristics of the filling. Although *Dido* differs from the other plays in containing no spoken dialogue, and may not strictly fall into this period, I shall for convenience' sake treat it with them. After dealing with the dramatic work there will remain the odes, the anthems and services, and the instrumental music.

THE THEATRE MUSIC.

We can scarcely hope to hear the bulk of the music for the theatre, as has been remarked, because of the worthlessness of the plays to which it is attached. Even *King Arthur, The Tempest, The Fairy Queen* and *Dioclesian* pieces are too fragmentary, disconnected, to be performed with any effect without scenery, costume, and some explanation in the way of dialogue. In *King Arthur* there are instrumental numbers to accompany action on the stage: without that action these numbers are meaningless. *King Arthur* was given at Birmingham some years ago, but it proved to be even more incoherent than the festival cantatas which our composers write to order: if the masque from *Timon* or *Dioclesian* had been inserted, few would have noticed the interpolation.

Dido and Aeneas is a different matter. It was very well performed by students some years since, and there is no reason why such an opera company as the Moody-Manners should not devote half an evening to it now and then. It is not long; excepting the solo parts, it is not difficult; it is entrancingly beautiful; properly staged, the dances of witches, etc., are fantastic and full of interest. For two hundred years every musician has admired Dido's lament, "When I am laid in Earth"; and indeed it is one of the most poignantly sorrowful and exquisitely beautiful songs ever composed. There are plenty of rollicking tunes, too, and the dance-pieces—*with the dancers*—are exhilarating and admirable for their purpose. The musicianship is as masterly as Purcell ever displayed. If Purcell composed the work before he was twenty-two he worked a miracle; and even if the date is ten years later it stands as a wonderful achievement. If we ask why he did not produce more real operas, there can be only one answer: the town did not care for them. The town went crazy over spectacular shows; even Dryden yielded to the town's taste; and there is no sign that Purcell cherished any particular private passion for opera as opera. He did his best for his paymaster. If there is no evidence hinting at his despising posterity, like Charles Lamb, or at any determination, also like Lamb, to write for antiquity, there is in his anthems and odes very considerable evidence that he was ready to write what his paymaster wanted written. We must bear in mind that downright bad taste, such as our present-day taste for such artistic infamies as the "Girls of This" and the "Belles of That," had not come into existence in Purcell's time. Purcell's contemporaries preferred his music to all other for the same reason that we prefer it to all other of his time—it was the best.

Dido, in pianoforte score, is generally accessible; only a few of the spoken play sets are as yet published, and they are ridiculously expensive. Let us not repine and give up hope. Some day that unheard-of thing an intelligent music publisher may be born into the world, and he may give Englishmen a trustworthy edition, at a fair price, of the works of England's greatest musician. Meantime, the reader must do as the writer did for some years—he must grub and laboriously copy in the British Museum, buying, when he can, the seventeenth-century edition of *Dioclesian* and the eighteenth-century editions of such works as *The Tempest* and *The Indian Queen*, and also the *Orpheus Britannicus*. To penetrate to Purcell's intention, to understand with what skill and force the intention is carried out, a knowledge of the music alone hardly suffices. I would not advise anything so terrible as an endeavour to read the whole of the plays, but at least *Boadicca, The Indian Queen, The Tempest, The Fairy Queen, Dioclesian* and *King Arthur* must be read; and it is worth while making an effort especially to grasp all the details of the masques. For themselves, few of the plays are worth reading; and, unluckily, the best of them have the least significant music. The others are neither serious plays nor good honest comedy; and a malicious fate willed that the very versions for which Purcell's aid was required were the worst of all—what little sense there was in the bad plays was destroyed when they were made into "operas" or "entertainments"—spectacular shows. Dryden was the best of the playwrights he was doomed to work with, and in *King Arthur* Dryden forgot about the aim and purpose of high drama, and concocted a hobgoblin pantomime interlarded with bravado concerning the greatness of Britain and Britons. *Dioclesian*, the first of Purcell's great theatre achievements, is even more stupid. The original play was *The Prophetess* of Beaumont and Fletcher, straightforward Elizabethan stodge and fustian: and if Betterton, who chose to maltreat it, was bent on making the very worst play ever written, it must be conceded that his success was nearly complete. It gets down to the plane of pure and sparkling idiocy that the world admires in, say, "The Merry Widow." Yet the masque afforded him opportunities of which he made splendid use. The overture is a noble piece of workmanship. There is a Handelian dignity without any bow-wow or stiffness, and the freshness and freedom are of a kind that Handel never attained to. Of course, it has no connection with the drama: it would serve for many another play just as well. What the theatre manager demanded of Purcell was a piece of music to occupy the audience before the curtain went up; and Purcell wrote it. There are songs and dances of a rare quality, and the biggest thing of all is the chorus, "Let all rehearse," which rivals Handel's "Fixed in his everlasting seat," a plain copy of it, down to many small points. Those who say Purcell had no influence upon his successors evidently know little either of Purcell's music or Handel's. Handel owed much to Purcell, and not least was the massive, direct way of dealing with the chorus, the very characteristic which has kept his oratorios so popular here and so unpopular abroad. Handel's mighty choral effects are English: he learnt from Purcell how to make them. It is true enough that Purcell learnt something from Carissimi; but Carissimi's effects are very often of that kind that look better on paper than they sound in performance. The variations over ground-basses are marvellously ingenious, but more marvellous than the ingenuity are the charming delicacy and expressiveness of the melodies woven in the upper parts. They are music which appeals direct to listeners who care nothing for technical problems. Some of the discords may sound a little odd to those who have been trained to regard the harmonic usages of the Viennese school as the standard of perfection. Dr. Burney thought them blunders resulting from an imperfect technique. Later a few words must be said on the subject, but let me for the present point out that Purcell was a master of the theory as well as of the practice of composition. He loved these discords, and deliberately wrote them; he could have justified them, and there is hardly one that we cannot justify. Purcell could write intricate fugues and canons without any "harsh progressions"; that he liked these for their own sake is obvious in numberless pieces where no laws of counterpoint compelled him to write this note rather than that. And though in the eyes of the theorists they are harsh, in the ears of all men they are sweet. The works of Purcell and of Mozart are the sweetest music ever composed, yet both composers filled their music with discords—"that give delight and hurt not."

In 1691 Purcell and Dryden did *King Arthur* together. The poet had by this time forsaken Monsieur Grabut, who had in his eyes at one time stood for all that was commendable in music. Grabut was more ingenious as a business man than as a musician, but not all his ingenuity served to prevent the English discovering that he could not write pleasing tunes and that Purcell could.[1] Whether Dryden felt any difference whatever between good and bad music I cannot say: he may have been like many of the poets, music-deaf (analogous to colour-blind). They are said to have been good friends, which I can well believe; and Dryden, when pursued by duns and men with writs and such implements of torture, is said to have stowed himself secretly in Purcell's room in the clock-tower of St. James's Palace, which one may believe or not, according to the mood of the moment. Anyhow, he seems to have been happy to work with Purcell, and for the spectacles in *King Arthur* they laid their two heads together and arranged some dazzling things which no one would care to see nowadays. *King Arthur* is almost as brilliant as *Dioclesian*, and contains some exceedingly patriotic songs. The stage in England always threatens most bloodshed to England's foes when those foes might seem to an impartial observer to be having the better of it. Only a few years ago the heroes of the music-hall menaced the Boers with unspeakable castigations when only they could be persuaded to leave off unaccountably thrashing our generals; and when Purcell wrote "Come if you Dare," and many another martial ditty, the time had not long passed when Van Tromp sailed up the Thames with a broom at his mast-head. All the same, "Come if you Dare" is a fine song; "Fairest Isles, all Isles excelling," is one of Purcell's loveliest thoughts, and the words are more boastful than ferocious; "Saint George, the Patron of our Isle," is brilliant and the words are innocuous. The masque element is not dumped into *King Arthur* altogether so shamelessly as in other cases; the whole play is a masque. Although there is a plot, the supernatural is largely employed, and nymphs, sirens, magicians, and what not, gave the composer notable chances. In the first act, the scene where the Saxons sacrifice to Woden and other of their gods, is the occasion for a chain of choruses, each short but charged with the true energy divine; then comes a "battle symphony," noisy but mild—a sham fight with blank cartridge; and after the battle the Britons sing a "song of victory," our acquaintance "Come if you Dare, the Trumpets Sound." The rest of the work is mainly enchantments and the like. More fairy-like music has never entered a musician's dreams than Philidel's "Hither this way," and the chorus which alternates with the solo part is as elfin, will-o'-th'-wispish, as anything of Mendelssohn. Mendelssohn is Purcell's only rival in such pictures. At the beginning of the celebrated Frost Scene, where Cupid calls up "thou genius of the clime" (the clime being Arctic), we get a specimen of Purcell's "word-painting":

[musical notation: "Stretch out thy la-zy limbs"]

This "word-painting," it must be noted, is of the very essence of Purcell's art, at any rate in vocal music. Suggestions came to him from the lines he was setting and determined the contours of his melody. He always does it, and never with ridiculous effect. Either the effect is dramatically right, as here; or impressive, as in "They that go down to the sea in ships"; or sublime as in "Full fathom five"; and whatever else it may be, it is always picturesque. The shivering chorus was an old idea in Purcell's time, but the sheer power of Purcell's music sets his use of it far above any other. It should be observed that none of the principals sing in these "operas": they couldn't. It is true that many singers, thorough musicians—Matthew Locke, for instance, and Purcell's own father—were also actors, or at least spoken of as actors. But it is evident they must have been engaged only for the singing parts, which were insignificant as far as the plots of the plays were concerned, though prominent enough in the spectacle or show, and therefore in the public gaze. When all the enchanters and genies, good and bad, have done their best or worst in *King Arthur*, the speaking characters finish up their share and the real play in spoken lines; then the singers and band wind up the whole entertainment in a style that was probably thought highly effective in the seventeenth century. After the last chorus—which begins as though the gathering were a Scotch one and we were going to have "Auld Lang Syne"—there is a final "grand dance," one of the composer's vigorous and elaborately worked displays on a ground-bass.

[1] Poor Grabut's fall was most lamentable. (His name, by the way, is spelt Grabu, or Grabut, or Grebus.) Pepys records that when "little Pelham Humfreys" returned from France he was bent on giving "Grebus" a lift out of his place. He most certainly did; and the case ought to be a warning to humbugs not to set their faith in princes. He had jockeyed competent men out of their places, and by 1674 he was himself ousted. He sank into miserable circumstances; and by the end of 1687 was dead. James II.—who was a much more honest paymaster than his brother—apparently paid up all arrears the Court owed him. His impudence must have been boundless; for he dared to measure himself not only against thorough workmen like Banister, but even men of genius like Humphries and Purcell. His audacity carried him in the end no further than a debtor's prison; and had he been paid only the value of his services, he might have died there.

Before making some general observations on the stage music, I wish to give a few instances of Purcell's power of drawing pictures and creating the very atmosphere of nature as he felt her. Let me begin with *The Tempest*. The music is of Purcell's very richest. Not even Handel in *Israel in Egypt* has given us the feeling of the sea with finer fidelity. Unluckily, to make this show Shakespeare's play was ruthlessly mangled, else Shakespeare's *Tempest* would never be given without Purcell's music. Many of the most delicate and exquisite songs are for personages who are not in the original at all, and no place can be found for their songs.

Two of Ariel's songs are of course known to everybody—"Full fathom five" and "Come unto these yellow sands," both great immortal melodies (in the second Shakespeare's words are doctored and improved). The first I have mentioned as a specimen of Purcell's "word-painting": there, at one stroke of immense imaginative power, we have the depths of the sea as vividly painted as in Handel's "And with the blast," or "The depths have covered them." Another exquisite bit of painting—mentioned in my first chapter—is repeated several times: the rippling sea on a calm day. It occurs first in Neptune's song, "While these pass o'er the deep"—

Next in Amphitrite's song, "Halcyon Days," a serenely lovely melody, we have

which is a variant. Then follows "See, the heavens smile," the opening of the vocal part of which I will quote for its elastic energy:

See, see, the heav-ens smile

In the instrumental introduction to the song this (and more) is first played by the viols a couple of octaves above, and after it we get our phrase:

—similarly harmonized (but major instead of minor) to the first example, and more fully worked out. In spite of incongruous masque or rather pantomime scenes the pervading atmosphere is sustained. One would say that Purcell got his inspiration by reading of Prospero's magic island, and never thought of Shadwell's stupid and boorish travesty.

The atmosphere of *The Fairy Queen* is not, to my mind, so richly odorous, so charged with the mystery and colour of pure nature, as that of *The Tempest*; but Purcell has certainly caught the patter of fairy footsteps and woven gossamer textures of melody. The score was lost for a couple of centuries, and turned up in the library of the Royal Academy of Music. In spite of being old-fashioned, it was not sufficiently out of date to remain there; so Mr. Shedlock edited it, and it has been published. *The Indian Queen* and *Bonduca* stand badly in need of careful editing—not in the spirit of one editor of *King Arthur* who, while declaring that he had altered nothing, stated that he had altered some passages to make them sound better. *The Indian Queen* contains the recitative "Ye twice ten hundred deities" and the song "By the croaking of the toad."

Purcell's forms are not highly organised. There are fugues, canons, exercises on a ground-bass, and many numbers are dances planned in much the same way as other people's dances, and songs differing only in their quality from folk-songs. Of form, as we use the word—meaning the clean-cut form perfected by Haydn—I have already asserted that there is none. This absence of form is held to be a defect by those who regard the Haydn form as an ideal—an ideal which had to be realised before there could be any music at all, properly speaking. But those of us who are not antediluvian academics know that form (in that sense) is not an end, but a means of managing and holding together one's material. In Purcell's music it is not needed. The torrent of music flowing from his brain made its own bed and banks as it went. Without modern form he wrote beautiful, perfectly satisfying music, which remains everlastingly modern. Neither did he feel the want of the mode of thematic development which we find at its ripest in Beethoven. As I have described in discussing the three-part sonatas, in movements that are not dances his invention is its own guide, though we may note that he employed imitation pretty constantly to knit the texture of the music close and tight. Many of the slow openings of the overture are antiphonal, passages sometimes being echoed, and sometimes a passage is continued by being repeated with the ups and downs of the melody inverted. Dozens of devices may be observed, but all are servants of an endless invention.

The variety of the songs and recitatives is wondrous. Purcell was one of the very greatest masters of declamation. In his recitative we are leagues removed from the "just accent" of Harry Lawes. It is passionate, or pathetic, or powerfully dramatic, or simply descriptive (in a way), or dignified, as the situation requires. "Let the dreadful engines" and "Ye twice ten hundred deities" have, strange to say, long been famous, in spite of their real splendour; and another great specimen is the command of Aeolus to the winds (in *King Arthur*)—"Ye blustering breezes ... retire, and let Britannia rise." The occasion is a pantomime, but Purcell used it for a master-stroke. He wrote every kind of recitative as it had never been written before in any language, and as it has not been written in English since. In the songs the words often suggest the melodic outline, as well as dictate the informing spirit. Many are rollicking, jolly; some touchingly expressive; most are purely English; a few rather Italian (old school) in manner. One can see what Purcell had gained by his study of Italian part-writing for strings, but he could not help penning picturesque phrases.

The dances are, of course, simple in structure. When they are in the form of passaglias they may be huge in design and effect. The grandest pieces are the overtures and choruses. The overtures are often very noble, but without pomposity or grandiloquence; indeed, they move as if unconscious of their own tremendous strength. One may hear half a dozen bars before a stroke reveals, as by a flash of lightning, the artistic purpose with which the parts are moving, and the enormous heat and energy that move them. When strength and sinew are wanted in the themes, they are there, and contrapuntal adaptability is there; but they are real living themes, not ossified or petrified formulas. Themes, part-writing and harmony are closely bound up in one another, and harmony is not the least important. Purcell liked daring harmonies, and they arise organically out of the firm march of individual parts. Excepting sometimes for a special purpose, he does not dump them down as accompaniment to an upper part. The "false relations" and "harsh progressions" of which the theorists prate do not exist for an unprejudiced ear. In writing the flattened leading note in one part against the sharpened in another he was merely following the polyphonists, and it sounds as well—nay, as beautiful—as any other discord, or the same discord on another degree of the scale.[2] This discord and his other favourites are beautiful in Purcell, and his determination to let them arise in an apparently unavoidable way from the collisions of parts, each going its defined road to its goal, must have determined the character of his part-writing. In spite of his remarks in Playford's book, it is plain that he looked at music horizontally as well as vertically, and constructed it so that it is good no matter which way it is considered. His counterpoint has a freedom and spontaneity not to be found in the music of the later contrapuntal, fugal, arithmetical school. Though he was pleased with musical ingenuities and worked plenty of them, he thought more of producing beautiful, expressive music than of mathematical skill. Handel frequently adopted his free contrapuntal style. Handel (and Bach, too) raised stupendous structures of ossified formulas, building architectural splendours of the materials that came to hand; but when Handel was picture-painting (as in *Israel*) and had a brush loaded with colour, he cared less for phrases that would "work" smoothly at the octave or twelfth than for subjects of the Purcell type.

[2] Since the above was written and in type I have read Mr. Ernest Walker's most interesting book, "Music in England," which contains a valuable chapter on the discords found in the music of Purcell and of earlier men.

THE ODES AND CHURCH MUSIC.

Some of the later odes are notable works. Perhaps the St. Cecilia ode of 1692 is, on the whole, the finest. Like the earlier works of the same class, in scheme the odes resemble the theatre sets, though, of course, there are neither dances nor curtain tunes. All that has been said about the stage music applies to them. The choruses are often very exhilarating in their go and sparkle and force, but I doubt whether Purcell had a larger number of singers for what we might call his concert-room works than in the theatre. The day of overgrown, or even fairly large, choruses and choral societies was not yet; many years afterwards Handel was content with a choir of from twenty to thirty. Had Purcell enjoyed another ten years of life, there is no saying how far he might have developed the power of devising massive choral designs, for we see him steadily growing, and there was no reason why the St. Cecilia ode of 1692 and the *Te Deum* and *Jubilate* should have remained as the culminating points. The overture to the 1692 ode is unusually fragmentary. I see no indication of any superior artistic aspiration in the fact that it consists of six short movements; rather, it seems to me that Purcell was, as ever, bent on pleasing his patrons—in this case with plenty of variety. Still, one movement leads naturally into the next, and scrappiness is avoided, and the music is of a high quality and full of vitality. Purcell frequently set a double bar at the end of a section, and makes two or more numbers where a modern composer would simply change the tempo and key-signature and go straight on, so that the scrappiness is only apparent. In this ode an instance occurs. There are fourteen numbers, but the last three are in reality one—a chorus, a quartet and a chorus repeating the opening bars of the first chorus. In a modern composition all would have run on with never a double bar. Purcell seems to have had no opportunity of designing another ode on the same broad scale as this. At any rate, he never did so, and the ode which did more than any other of his achievements, save, perhaps, the *Yorkshire Feast-Song* of 1689, to convince his contemporaries of his greatness, abides as his noblest monument in this department of music.

Just as by writing music for plays which will never be acted again Purcell cut off his appeal to after generations of play-goers, so by writing anthems on a model sadly out of place in a sacred service he hid himself from future church-goers. King Charles liked his Church music as good as you like, but lively at all costs, and the royal mind speedily wearying of all things in turn, he wished the numbers that made up an anthem to be short. So Purcell wasted his time and magnificent thematic material on mere strings of scrappy, jerky sections. The true Purcell touch is on them all, but no sooner has one entered fairly into the spirit of a passage than it is finished. Instrumental interludes—if, indeed, they can be called interludes, for they are as important as the vocal sections—abound, and might almost be curtain-tunes from the plays. Nothing can be done to make these anthems of any use in church. Eighteenth and nineteenth century editors have laid clumsy fingers on them, curtailing the instrumental bits; but nothing is gained by this rough-and-ready process, as no Purcell has ever appeared to lengthen the vocal portions. As Purcell left the anthems, so we must leave them—exquisite fragments that we may delight in, but that are of no use in the service for which they were composed. Still, this does not apply to them all; at least twenty of the finest are splendidly schemed, largely designed, and will come into our service lists more frequently when English Church musicians climb out of the bog in which they are now floundering. They are full, if I may use the phrase, of pagan-religious feeling. Purcell's age was not a devotional age, and Purcell himself, though he wrote Church music in a serious, reverential spirit, could not detach himself from his age and get back to the sublime religious ecstasy of Byrde. He seizes upon the texts to paint vivid descriptive pieces; he thrills you with lovely passages or splendours of choral writing; but he did not try to express devotional moods that he never felt. A mood very close to that of religious ecstasy finds a voice in "Thou knowest, Lord, the Secrets of our Hearts"—the mood of a man clean rapt away from all earthly affairs, and standing face to face, alone, with the awful mystery of "the infinite and eternal energy from which all things proceed." It is plain, direct four-part choral writing, but the accent is terrible in its distinctness. At Queen Mary's funeral (we can judge from Tudway's written reflections) the audience was overwhelmed, and we may believe it. A more elaborately wrought and longer piece of work is the setting of the Latin Psalm, "Jehova, quam multi sunt." It is the high-water mark of all Church music after the polyphonists. By Church music I mean music written for the Church, not necessarily religious music. The passage at "Ego cubui et dormivi" is sublime, Purcell's discords creating an atmosphere of strange beauty, almost unearthly, and that yields to the unspeakable tenderness of the naïve phrase at the words, "Quia Jehovah sustentat me." The *Te Deum* was until recently known only by Dr. Boyce's perversion. Dr. Boyce is reputed to have been an estimable moral character, and it is to be hoped he was, for that is the best we can say of him. He was a dunderheaded worshipper and imitator of Handel. Thinking that Purcell had tried to write in the Handelian bow-wow, and for want of learning had not succeeded; thinking also that he, Dr. Boyce, being a musical doctor, had that learning, he took Purcell's music in hand, and soon put it all right— turned it, that is, into a clumsy, forcible-feeble copy of Handel. One could scarcely recognise Purcell so blunderingly disguised. However, we now know better, and the *Te Deum* stands before us, pure Purcell, in all its beauty, freshness, sheer strength, and, above all, naïve direct mode of utterance. It looks broken, but does not sound broken. Purcell simply went steadily through the canticle, setting each verse as he came to it to the finest music possible. The song "Vouchsafe, O Lord," is an unmatched setting of the words for the solo alto, full of very human pathos; and some of the choral parts are even more brilliant than the odes. The *Jubilate* is almost as fine; but we must take both, not as premature endeavours to work Handelian wonders, but as the full realisations of a very different ideal.

THE FOUR-PART SONATAS.

In the last sonatas (of four parts, published 1697) the Italian influence is even more marked than in the earlier ones. The general plan is the same, but more effect is got out of the strings without the management of the parts ceasing to be Purcellian. We get slow and quick movements in alternation, or if two slow ones are placed together they differ in character. Variety was the main conscious aim. The notion of getting a unity of the different movements of a sonata occurred to no one until long after. We learn nothing by comparing the various sequences of the movements in the different sonatas, for the simple reason that there is nothing to learn, and it may be remarked that for the same reason elaborate analysis of the arrangement of the sections which make up the overtures is wasted labour. The essential unity of Purcell's different sets of pieces is due to something that lies deep below the surface of things—he was guided only by his unfailing intuition.

In these ten sonatas we have Purcell, the composer of pure music, independent of words and stage-scenes, at his ripest and fullest. The subjects are full of sinew, energy, colour; the technique of the fugues is impeccable; the intensity of feeling in some of these slow movements of his is sometimes almost startling when one of his strokes suddenly proclaims it. There are sunny, joyous numbers, too, robust, jolly tunes, as healthy and fresh as anything in the theatre pieces. The "Golden" sonata is, after all, a fair representative. If the last movement seems—as most of the finales of all the composers until Beethoven do seem—a trifle light and insignificant after the almost tragic seriousness of the largo, we must bear in mind that it was very frequently part of Purcell's design to have a cheerful ending. Unfortunately, there is no good edition of the sonatas. They are chamber music, and never were intended to be played in a large room. They should be played in a small room, and the pianist—for harpsichords are woefully scarce to-day—should fill in his part from the figured bars simply with moving figurations, neither plumping down thunderous chords nor (as one editor lately proposed) indulging in dazzling show passages modelled on Moscheles and Thalberg. Properly played, no music is more delightful.

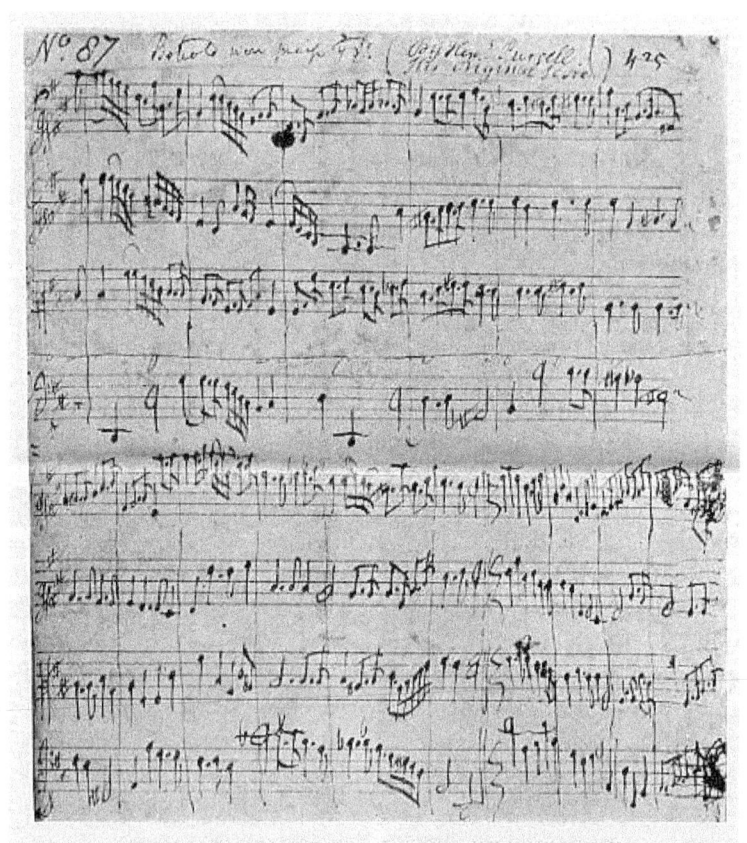

PART OF THE AUTOGRAPH SCORE OF PURCELL'S ANTHEM
"BEHOLD, NOW PRAISE THE LORD."

(In the British Museum.)

CHAPTER V

It is impossible to touch on more than a few characteristic examples of Purcell's achievement. There are many charming detached songs; the *Harpsichord Lessons* contain exquisite things. There is also a quantity of unpublished sacred and secular music of high value.

When Purcell died, on November 21, 1695, he was busy with the music for Tom d'Urfey's *Don Quixote* (part iii.), being helped by one Eccles, who enjoyed a certain mild fame in his day. The last song, "set in his sicknesse," was a song supposed to be sung by a mad woman, "From rosy bowers." The recitative is magnificent; two of the sections in tempo are fine, especially the second; the last portion is meant to depict raving lunacy, and does so. It is by no means one of Purcell's greatest efforts, and he apparently had no notion of making a dramatic exit from this world. If the doctors knew what disease killed him, they never told. The professional libeller of the dead, Hawkins, speaks of dissipations and late hours: and he would have us believe that he left his family in poverty. As a matter of fact, Mrs. Purcell was left quite well off, and was able to give her son Edward a good education. She had also property to bequeath when she died in 1706. Purcell worked so hard that he cannot have had time for the life of tavern-rioting that Hawkins invented. All we know is that he died, and that his death was a tragic loss to England. A few days later he was buried in Westminster Abbey, to the sound of his own most solemn music. A tablet to his memory was placed near the grave, and the inscription on it is said to have been written by the wife of Sir Robert Howard, author of the *Indian Queen* and other forgotten master-works. The light of English music had gone out, though few at the moment realised it, for Dr. Blow and Eccles and others went on composing music which was thought very good. But the light had gone, and it was not Handel who extinguished it. Handel did not come to England for fifteen years, and during that fifteen years not a single composition worthy of being placed within measurable distance of Purcell's average work fell from an English pen. Purcell was by no means forgotten all at once. The four-part sonatas were issued in 1697, the *Harpsichord Lessons* in 1696; the *Choice Ayres for the Theatre*—selections from the stage music—came out in 1697; the first book of the *Orpheus Britannicus* appeared in 1698, and a second edition of it in 1706; the second book of the same appeared in 1702, and a second edition in 1711; while a third edition of both books was published as late as 1721, when Handel had been settled in England some years. The fame of our last great musician survived him for quite a long time, as things go. That the re-issue of his works was not due alone to the energy of his widow is clear, for she died in 1706.

It is indeed mournful to contemplate the havoc disease and death play with the might-have-beens of men and of causes. Pelham Humphries, an unmistakable genius, was carried away at twenty-seven; Henry Purcell, one of the mightiest of the world's masters of music, died at the age of thirty-seven, only two years older than his peer in genius, Mozart. Yet he left a glorious record, and his days must have been glorious. Men like Purcell do not create music such as theirs by blind instinct, as a cat catches mice. A mighty brain and mightier heart must have worked with passionate energy, the fires must have burnt at an unbroken white heat, to produce so much unsurpassable music in so short a time. The qualities we find in the music were in him before they got into the music; all that we can enjoy he enjoyed first. He had, too, a high destiny to work out, and he knew it. Thomas Tudway said he was ambitious to exceed everyone of his time. To the last he laboured unceasingly, and if he died, as has been suspected, of consumption, there is no trace of the fever of ill-health nor any morbidity in his creations. They are charged with energy—often elemental, volcanic energy that nothing can resist; and at its lowest, the energy is the energy of robust health and a keen appetite. That energy carried him far beyond the modest goal he thought of, exceeding his fellows. He won the topmost heights within the reach of man. The old polyphonists he never tried to rival, but in the style of music he wrote no composer has gone or can go higher than he. A wiseacre has said that he left a sterile monument. It may be that monuments in the British Museum blow and blossom and reproduce their kind: outside they do not. If the wiseacre meant that Purcell did not leave, as Haydn and Mozart undoubtedly did, a form in which dullards may compose until the world is sick, then the wiseacre is right But the inventors and perfecters of forms have not always wrought an unmitigated good. If Haydn left a fruitful monument in the symphony, and Handel in his particular form of oratorio, and if we thankfully praise Haydn and Handel for these their benefits, must we not also blame Haydn for the dull symphonies that nearly drove Schumann and Wagner mad, and Handel for the countless copies of his oratorios that rendered stupid, dull, and insensible to the beauty of music those generations that have attended our great musical festivals? The spirit of Purcell's work and its technique did not die with Purcell: the spirit of much of Handel's music, and certainly of his masterpiece, *Israel in Egypt*, is Purcell's; and eighteenth-century contrapuntist though Handel was, much of his technique came from Purcell. Rightly regarded, Purcell's monument is anything but sterile. Felix Mottl, worried to exasperation by stale laments for Mozart's premature death, once lifted up his voice and thanked God for Mozart, the Heaven-sent man. In the same spirit we may be thankful for Purcell. In his music we have the full and perfect expression of all that was fair and sweet and healthy in this England of ours; "all thoughts, all passions, all delights," that our English nature is capable of find a voice in his music—if only we will take the trouble to listen to it. He is neglected, it is true, but he is immortal: time is nothing: he can wait. If our age neglects him, his age neglected Shakespeare. Shakespeare's time came; Purcell's cannot be for ever delayed.

LIST OF WORKS.

Music for over fifty dramas, including *Dioclesian* (1690), *King Arthur* (1692), *Bonduca*, *The Indian Queen*, and *The Tempest* (1695).

Over two hundred songs, duets, catches, etc.

Twelve sonatas of three parts (1683), ten of four parts (published 1697). *Harpsichord Lessons* (published 1696). A number of fantasias for strings.

About one hundred anthems; a quantity of sacred music apparently not for Church use; *Te Deum* and *Jubilate in D*; complete service in B flat; evening service in G minor.

www.ingramcontent.com/pod-product-compliance
Ingram Content Group UK Ltd.
Pitfield, Milton Keynes, MK11 3LW, UK
UKHW041019120225
455007UK00004B/206

9 789362 927552